AF448395

Fun Facts, Quotes and Jokes about MOTHERS

Danny De Nero

No part of this book may be reproduced or transmitted in any form or by any means, electronic or mechanical, including photocopying, photographing or by any information storage retrieval system, without the written permission from the publisher.

Entire book designed by Danny De Nero.

Copyright 2024. All rights reserved.

Note: Any facts presented in this book are accurate at the time of publication. However, in time new information may impact the accuracy of some facts. The author and publisher are not responsible for any fact changes that may emerge after the publication date.

m

Contents

FACTS about

MOTHERS

Mother Earth: In Greek mythology, Gaia, or Mother Earth, was the first goddess. She created herself out of primordial chaos. She also created Earth and the universe.

Origin of the word "Mother": The word "mother" comes from the Latin word "mater", which means "origin" or "source".

Ancient Greece and Rome: The ancient Greeks and Romans had festivals to honour the mother goddesses Rhea and Cybele, who were associated with fertility, nature, and protection.

M

Mothering Sunday: In the 16th century, the Christian church in Europe established Mothering Sunday, which was the fourth Sunday of Lent.

On this day, people would return to their mother church, the main church in their region, and honour the Virgin Mary.

Years later, Mothering Sunday would be a day when domestic servants were given a day off to visit their church with their family members. Often this was one of the few times when the whole family were able to be together, so the day was fit for celebration.

First Mother's Day in the USA: The modern American version of Mother's Day was initiated by Anna Jarvis, who organized the first Mother's Day service of worship at St. Andrew's Methodist Church in Grafton, West Virginia, on May 10, 1908.

She wanted to commemorate her mother, Ann Reeves Jarvis, who was a peace activist and a social reformer.

M

She also wanted to promote the role of mothers in society and advocate for their rights and welfare.

She campaigned for Mother's Day to be recognized as a national holiday, which was achieved in 1914 by President Woodrow Wilson.

However, she later regretted the commercialisation of the holiday and tried to stop it, unsuccessfully.

Babies in Bali: The Balinese believe that a newborn is accompanied at birth by four sibling spirits who safeguarded it whilst in the womb. These spirits manifest in the placenta, amniotic fluid, the blood, and vernix caseosa (the white creamy biofilm covering the skin of the foetus).

When a baby is born, a ceremony takes place where the placenta is cleaned, placed in a sealed container, wrapped in white cloth, and buried outside of the home.

The spirit in the placenta serves as a guardian until the child loses their first tooth, while the other three aspects are believed to continue as protective spirits throughout life.

Seen as divine beings descended from heaven, a newborn baby's feet cannot touch the ground for 210 days. When they do, it symbolizes their crossing over to the earth realm.

M

In **Ethiopia**, there is a festival called Antrosht, which is dedicated to mothers and is held at the end of the rainy season.

Families gather together and prepare a large meal, with daughters bringing vegetables and cheese, and sons bringing meat.

Finland – equal start to life: Since the 1930s, the Finish government issues mothers with a care package – a box of essential baby items – known internationally as the Finish Baby Box.

Originally created for low-income families to give all babies an equal start in life, it became available to all moms from 1949.

All expectant mothers who live in Finland have access to the maternity package, with some reasonable rules in place.

Over the years, the box contents have changed, and today mothers can choose to forgo the box for a cash grant. However, most opt for the box as its contents are worth far more.

M

The box contains essential items like nappy cream, teething toys, mittens, baby grows, bibs, a snowsuit and even condoms!

Also in the box is a box-sized mattress and blanket, so the box can double-up as a crib.

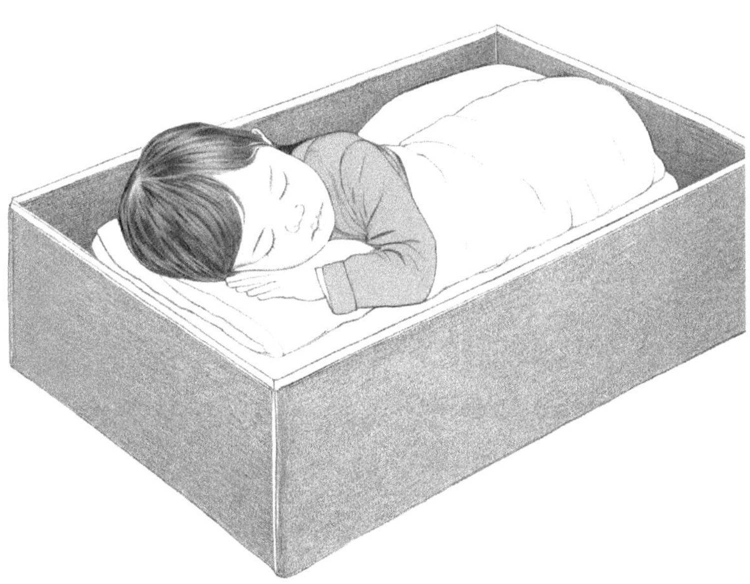

In **India**, there is a 10-day festival called Durga Puja, which honours the goddess of mothers, Durga. Families prepare food, gifts, and decorations for the festival, which is also a time for family reunions. The festival is usually held in October.

M

Oldest mother in the world on record:
Erramatti Mangamma, born in
1946, currently holds the record for being
the oldest living mother to give birth.

On 5th September 2019, she gave birth to twin
girls at the age of 73, through in-vitro
fertilisation in the city of Hyderabad, India
(she had a caesarean section).

Prior to her, the oldest mother in the world
was Daljinder Kaur (also from India), who
gave birth to a son in 2016 at the age of 72.

Youngest mother in the world on record: The youngest mother in the world is Lina Medina from Peru. She gave birth to a son in 1939 at the age of five years, seven months and 21 days by caesarean section.

Medina's son weighed 2.7 kg at birth (6 pounds and 0.43 stone) and was named Gerardo after her doctor. Medina had a rare condition called precocious puberty, which caused her to start menstruating at the age of three.

Up until the age of 10, Gerardo was raised to believe Medina was his sister. He grew up generally healthy.

He died of a bone disease aged 40.

M

Most children born to one mother: The most children born to one mother is 69, according to the Guinness World Records.

The mother was Valentina Vassilyeva, a peasant from Russia, who lived in the 18th century.   She had 16 pairs of twins, seven sets of triplets, and four sets of quadruplets.

Longest interval between births: The longest interval between two births from the same mother is 41 years and 185 days, according to the Guinness World Records.

The mother is Elizabeth Ann Buttle from Wales, who gave birth to a daughter in 1956 and a son in 1997. She was 19 years old when she had her first child and 60 years old when she had her second child.

M

Longest human pregnancy: Most healthy human pregnancies last around 280 days, with a normal variation between 259 and 287 days.

In 1945, Beaulah Hunter gave birth to a baby girl in Los Angeles after a 375-day pregnancy, at age 25. She was pregnant for over a year and was more than 100 days overdue.

Her daughter, Penny Diana, was born on 21st February 1945 weighing 3.14 kg – a healthy baby.

Years later, in 2016, a Chinese woman claimed she was pregnant for 17 months. However, she refused to produce an ultrasound as proof, so medical experts have doubts about the authenticity of her claim.

M

-15-

Longest nursing dependency: A mother orangutan typically nurses her babies for six to seven years.

This is the longest known child/mother nursing dependence of any mammal on earth.

Octuplets: The first recorded case of octuplets was in 1967 in Mexico, but sadly none of the babies survived.

The first set of octuplets to survive past infancy was born in 2009 in the United States to Nadya Suleman, who became known as "Octomom".

She had six other children prior to her octuplets. That's potentially fourteen sets of helping hands around the house!

M

Nonuplets: The first (and only known) incidence of nonuplets surviving birth was in May 2021 in Casablanca, Morocco.

On 6 May 2021, Associated Press announced the delivery of nine children born to Halima Cisse. Halima lived in Mali and doctors thought she was pregnant with seven babies.

The Mali government provided financial support for her to be flown to Casablanca and cared for there.

Her nine babies were born at 30 weeks gestation. She and her babies returned to her home country, Mali, after 19 months in Morocco.

Identical twins: The chances of giving birth to identical twins are relatively consistent worldwide, occurring in about 1 in 250 pregnancies.

Sharks: In certain shark species, females reproduce through a process called parthenogenesis, where eggs develop without fertilization.

M

The **Surinam toad** is unique in that the mother carries her eggs on her back, embedded in the skin until they hatch.

Brain fog: Many women report short term memory loss during pregnancy and early motherhood. A scientific study was conducted in 2016 to analyse brain scans before and after pregnancy.

Researchers discovered that mothers experience a reduction in grey matter during pregnancy, and these changes persist for at least two years. Interestingly, women who exhibited greater grey matter losses tended to score higher on their attachment to their child.

Cannibal hamsters: First-time mother hamsters may eat their babies if they feel threatened by them, if they need extra nutrients after giving birth or of the baby hamsters are deformed or ill.

Bats: Mother bats carry their pups while foraging, often utilizing their wings as a makeshift sling.

Sea turtles: Female sea turtles return to the same beach where they were born to lay their eggs, following an instinctive nesting behaviour.

M

Seahorses: After a mating dance, female seahorses deposit their eggs into a specialized pouch on the male's abdomen, where he carries and nurtures the developing embryos. The pregnancy lasts between 10 and 30 days (depending on the species) and the male seahorse can give birth up to 2,000 babies. Typically, five or less infant seahorses in every 1,000 survive to adulthood.

Dolphins: About two weeks before they give birth, bottlenose dolphins whistle more often. This is thought to be an attempt by mother dolphin to teach baby her unique sound signature whistle.

The sound "ma": The most common name for mothers in the world is "mama" or a variation of it, such as "mami", "mamma", "ma", "mom" or "mum".
This is because the sound "ma" is one of the easiest sounds for babies to make.

m

Octopus – ultimate commitment: The mission of a female octopus is to have just one successful brood in her lifetime. She will lay around 200,000 eggs and care for them without leaving them, almost starving to death.

Some octopus mothers even ingest their own arms rather than leaving the eggs for food.

The last thing a mother octopus does for her young when they are ready to hatch is to blow them through her siphon and disperse them.

By the time the babies hatch and float in plankton blooms, the mother is so weak and often falls prey to predators or just does from starvation and malnourishment.

Largest mammal babies: Blue whale:

Blue whales are the largest (known) living mammals on earth.

Their calves are born at 5,000 to 6,000 pounds (2,250kg to 2,700). They can grow up to 200 pounds per day (approximately 90kg per day) until they reach full size at approximately 400,000 pounds (180,000 kg).

To nurse their calves, blue whale mothers must produce around 50 gallons (190 litres) of milk per day.

As a comparison, human mothers produce around a litre of milk per day (variation depending on several factors).

M

Babysitting: Female meerkats in a group share nursing duty between themselves.

They take turns serving as sentinels to watch for predators while the others forage.

Sea otters. Sea otter mothers wrap their pups in kelp to keep them anchored while they dive for food.

Koalas: A mother koala will feed her baby her own faeces. This is because the baby hasn't developed the intestinal bacteria to help detoxify poisonous eucalyptus leaves, which are a koala's primary diet.

Skin care: Research shows that a mother holding her premature baby closely against her chest for a few uninterrupted hours a day delivers health benefits to the baby.

This practice is sometimes called "kangaroo care" and is practiced at an increasing number of neonatal care units in hospitals. Studies have shown that this can help premature babies improve their immune system, increase their pain threshold and gain weight faster.

Maternal bonding: A foetal heart races faster when hearing its mothers voice, compared to anyone else's voice.

The hormone oxytocin, often called the "love hormone," plays a key role in maternal bonding and is released during childbirth and breastfeeding.

QUOTES about MOTHERS

The art of mothering is to teach the art of living to children.

-Elaine Heffner

The influence of a mother in the lives of her children is beyond calculation.

-James E. Faust

Motherhood is near to divinity. It is the highest, holiest service to be assumed by mankind.

-Howard W. Hunter

Motherhood is the exquisite inconvenience of being another person's everything.

-Unknown

When your children are teenagers, it's important to have a dog so that someone in the house is happy to see you.

– Nora Ephron

Motherhood:

All love begins and ends there.

-Robert Browning

A mother's love is patient and forgiving when all others are forsaking, it never fails or falters, even though the heart is breaking.

– Helen Rice

When your mother asks, 'Do you want a piece of advice?' it is a mere formality. It doesn't matter if you answer yes or no. You're going to get it anyway.

– Erma Bombeck

There's no way to be a perfect mother and a million ways to be a good one.

– Jill Churchill

Kids are challenging. Wine is necessary.

–Kelly Clarkson

A mother's love is like a beacon, lighting up the future but reflected also on the past in the guise of fond memories.

- Honore de Balzac

The heart of a mother is a deep abyss at the bottom of which you will always find forgiveness.

-Honore de Balzac

I want my children to have all the things I couldn't afford. Then I want to move in with them."

-Phyllis Diller

M

My mother's menu consisted of two choices: Take it or leave it.

–Buddy Hackett

Stop saying 'we're pregnant.' You're not pregnant. Do you have to squeeze a watermelon–sized person out of your lady hole? No.

–Mila Kunis

Youth fades; love droops; the leaves of friendship fall; a mother's secret hope outlives them all.

– Oliver Wendell Holmes

Children are like crazy, drunken small people in your house.

-Julie Bowen

Having children just puts the whole world into perspective. Everything else just disappears.

-Kate Winslet

M

I am sure that if the mothers of various nations could meet, there would be no more wars.

-E. M. Forster

Motherhood is tough. If you just want a wonderful little creature to love, you can get a puppy.

- Barbara Walters

Motherhood has a very humanizing effect.
Everything gets reduced to essentials.

–Meryl Streep

A mother is a person who, seeing there are only
four pieces of pie for five people, promptly
announces she never did care for pie."

–Tenneva Jordan

If evolution really works, how come mothers only
have two hands?

–Milton Berle

A mother's love is the fuel that enables a normal human being to do the impossible.

- Marion C. Garretty

God could not be everywhere, and therefore he made mothers.

- Rudyard Kipling

Motherhood is the biggest gamble in the world. It is the glorious life force. It's huge and scary – it's an act of infinite optimism.

- Gilda Radner

The only love that I really believe in is a mother's love for her children.

- Karl Lagerfeld

M

Sleep at this point is just a concept, something I'm looking forward to investigating in the future.

-Amy Poehler

I believe the choice to become a mother is the choice to become one of the greatest spiritual teachers there is.

-Oprah

Mothers hold their children's hands for a short while, but their hearts forever.

-Unknown

As long as a woman can look ten years younger

than her own daughter,

she is perfectly satisfied.

-Oscar Wilde

To describe my mother would be to write about a hurricane in its perfect power. Or the climbing, falling colours of a rainbow.

- Maya Angelou

If I were asked to define Motherhood, I would have defined it as Love in its purest form. Unconditional love.

- Revathi Sankaran

For when a child is born, the mother also is born again.

-Unknown

The best place to cry is in a mother's arms.

- Jodi Picoult

A mother is she who can take the place of all others but whose place no one else can take.

-Cardinal Meymillod

Life began with waking up and loving

my mother's face.

-George Elliot

The most important thing a father can do

for his children is to

love their mother.

-Theodore Hesburgh

Children are the anchors

that hold a mother to life.

-Sophocles

The mother's heart is

the child's schoolroom.

-Henry Ward Beecher

Mother: the most beautiful word

on the lips of mankind.

-Kahlil Gibran

m

-47-

We are born of love;

love is our mother.

-Rumi

JOKES about MOTHERS

M

There's nothing quite like being told I'm wrong by someone who depends on me for food, clothing, and shelter.

Son: "Mom, stop making jokes. You're not funny."
Mom: "I made you, didn't I?"

Don't be so hard on yourself; the mom in ET had an alien living in her house for weeks and didn't notice.

Mother: "That's it. We're selling the kids on eBay."

Father: "Don't be silly! We made them."

Mother: "OK, we'll sell them on Etsy."

You know you're a mom when picking up another human to smell their butt isn't only normal, but necessary.

M

Son: "Mom, can I have $20?"

Mom: "Does it look like I am made of money?"

Son: "Well, isn't that what M-O-M stands for?"

What did the mom say to her teenager

when she asked her to keep a secret?

Mum's the word.

Why did the mother always carry a pencil?

To draw the line

when her kids misbehaved!

Whoever wrote the song,

"Easy Like Sunday Morning"

...did not have kids.

Son: "Mom, what's a weekend?"
Mom: "I don't know, sweetheart,

I haven't had one since you were born."

Why did the mother always have a flashlight?

In case her kids needed a "bright" idea!

What did the baby corn say to the mama corn?
Where's Pop corn?

M

Children: You spend the first 2 years of their life teaching them to walk and talk.

Then you spend the next 16 years telling them to sit down and shut up.

Being a mom to one or more teenagers will make you understand why some animals eat their young.

M

My kids asked me what it

was like to be a mom.

So, I woke them up at 3 a.m.

demanding to know

where my lucky sock was.

Licked a dark smear off my finger,

and then thought,

"Phew it's chocolate."

Boy: "My mom is having a new baby."
Girl: "What's wrong with the old one?"

M

Daughter: "Mom, what's it like to have the greatest daughter in the world?"

Mother: "I don't know, ask your grandma!"

Showering as a mom should be an Olympic sport:

Everyone's yelling your name, you have to beat the clock,

and you hardly ever win a medal.

Why did the mother cross the road?

To get some peace and quiet!

Science teacher:

"When is the boiling point reached?"

Student:

"When my mother sees my report card!"

M

Daughter: "Mom, I need my personal space!"

Mom: "You came out of *my* personal space!

A police recruit was asked during the exam, "What would you do if you had to arrest your own mother?"

He said, "Call for backup."

What do you call a small mom?

Minimum.

How many moms does it take to screw in a lightbulb? One, OBVIOUSLY... and SHE has to do it or else it won't get done.

M

There is a legend that if you take a shower and scream "Mom" three times, a nice lady appears with the towel you forgot.

Kid: "What's a man?"
Dad: "A man is someone who is responsible and cares for their family."
Kid: "I hope one day I can be a man just like mom!"

"Mike, can't you paint on walls like other children? Do you have any idea how hard it is to get that stuff off the ceiling?"

— Michelangelo's mother

Baby snake: "Mommy, are we poisonous?"
Mommy snake: "Yes, son. Why?"
Baby snake: "I just bit my tongue!"

Johhny: Larry's mother had four children...
Three were named North, South and West.
What was her other child's name?
Bobbie: East?
Johhny: No. Larry.

M

"Humpty, If I've told you once, I've told you a hundred times *not to sit on that wall.* But would you listen to me? No!"

— Humpty Dumpty's Mother

www.ingramcontent.com/pod-product-compliance
Lightning Source LLC
Chambersburg PA
CBHW061633130726
47996CB00003B/1262